Fantastic Fiction

Columbus, OH • Chicago, IL • Redmond, WA

The **McGraw·Hill** Companies

The Independent Reading Books

The *Independent Reading Books* are reading books that fill the need for easy-to-read stories for the primary grades. The appeal of these stories will encourage independent reading at the early grade levels.

The stories focus on the Dolch 220 Basic Sight Vocabulary and the 95 Common Nouns. Beyond these lists, the books use about three new words per page.

This series was prepared under the direction and supervision of Edward W. Dolch, Ph.D.

This revision was prepared under the direction and supervision of Eleanor Dolch LaRoy and the Dolch Family Trust.

SRAonline.com

 SRA

Copyright © 2005 by The Dolch Trust.

Send all inquiries to:
SRA/McGraw-Hill
8787 Orion Place
Columbus, OH 43240-4027

Printed in the United States of America.

ISBN 0-07-602523-3

2 3 4 5 6 7 8 9 BSF 12 11 10 09 08 07 06 05

The McGraw-Hill Companies

Table of Contents

The Little Red Hen and the Fox

Once upon a time a little red hen lived in a house upon a hill. And far down the hill, under a big, big stone, lived a fox and his mother.

One day the fox said to his mother, "I would like a chicken to eat."

"The little red hen lives up on the hill," said his mother. "She would be very good to eat."

The fox laughed and said, "Let us put the pot on the fire. I am going up the hill to get the little red hen."

And the fox went up the hill with a big bag to get the little red hen.

The little red hen had on her blue apron. She was cleaning her house. She had all the doors and windows open.

When the fox got to the little red hen's house, he walked right in the door.

"Good morning, Little Red Hen," said the fox. "I have come up the hill to see you."

The little red hen did not know what to do. She did not like the fox because the fox liked to eat chickens.

But she said, "Good morning, Fox. You must be tired after your long walk up the hill. Will you sit down by the fire?"

The fox sat down in a big chair. And the little red hen went out to get a stick of wood for the fire. When she came back, the fox looked as if he were sleeping. But when the little red hen went to put the stick of wood on the fire, the fox jumped up. He put a bag right over the little red hen. He took a string out of his pocket and put it around and around the top of the bag.

"Now I will have a little red hen to eat," the fox said as he laughed to himself. And he put the bag on his back and started down the hill.

It was a long, long walk down the hill. Soon the fox was very tired. He sat down under a tree, and he put the bag down on the grass. Then the fox went to sleep.

The little red hen had been thinking and thinking. She had to get out of that bag. Now the little red hen had some sewing scissors in the pocket of her blue apron. When the fox put the bag on the grass, she took her sewing scissors out of her apron pocket and cut the bag. Then the little red hen got out of the bag.

She looked all around. She saw a stone as big as she was. She put the stone into the bag. She took some of the string from around the top of the bag and sewed up the bag where she had cut it with the scissors.

Then the little red hen ran up the hill to her house as fast as she could go.

Pretty soon the fox opened his eyes. "My, my," said the fox to himself, "I must take this chicken to my mother. She will be wanting to eat it."

The fox got up and put the bag on his back and went down the hill to his house.

"Did you bring the little red hen?" asked his mother.

"She is here in the bag," said the fox. "Do you have the pot of hot water to put her in?"

"Yes," said his mother, "let us put the little red hen into the pot of hot water."

"I will hold the bag," said the fox. "You take the string off the top of the bag. Then we will both put the little red hen into the pot."

But into the pot went the big stone, not the little red hen. And the hot water went all over the fox and his mother.

Oh, how they ran around and around! And never again did that fox go up the hill to get the little red hen.

The Cap That Father Made

There was once a little boy called Andrew. One day his father made him a new red cap. The cap was so pretty. Andrew had never seen a hat like it. And it was his very own.

Everyone told Andrew that he looked very fine in his new red cap. Andrew put on his new red cap and went for a walk down the road.

As Andrew was going down the road, he saw a big boy.

"What a fine red cap you have," said the big boy. "I will give you my cat if you will give me your red cap."

Now Andrew wanted a cat. But he could not give away the new red cap his father had made.

"No, no," said Andrew, "I cannot give you my new red cap." And Andrew walked on down the road.

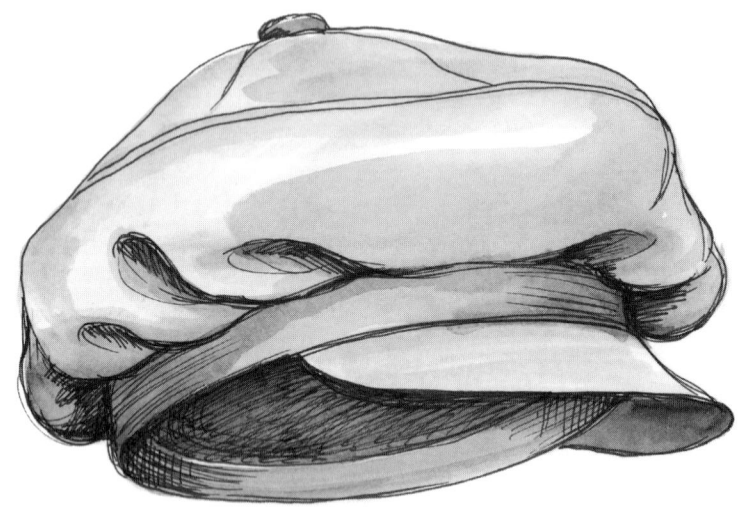

Before long Andrew saw an old woman. The old woman called to Andrew, "Andrew, my boy, what a fine red cap you have on your head."

"Yes," said Andrew. "My father made it for me."

"And where are you going, Andrew, my boy, with that fine red cap upon your head?" asked the old woman.

"I think," said Andrew, "I will go to see the king. I want him to see the new red cap my father made for me." And Andrew walked on down the road.

Pretty soon Andrew got to the palace where the king lived. Andrew was going to walk right in the door, but the soldiers by the door would not let him in.

"Who are you?" the soldiers said. "Why do you want to go into the king's palace?"

"I am Andrew," said the little boy, "and I want to show the king the new red cap my father made for me."

But the soldiers only laughed and would not let him into the palace.

Just then the princess walked by. She saw the little boy at the door of the palace. "Who are you?" asked the princess.

"I am Andrew," said the little boy, "and I want to show the king the new red cap my father made for me."

"Come with me," said the princess, "and
we will go and find the king."

So Andrew and the princess walked into
the palace hand in hand. The palace was a
big, big palace, and they walked and
walked.

At last they got to a big room. And in the
room was a long table.

At the head of the table sat the queen in a gold chair. And on the table were big red apples and good white cakes to eat.

"Mother," said the princess, "this is Andrew. He has come to show us his new red cap."

"Come, Andrew," said the queen, "and sit on this chair by me."

Andrew sat on a gold chair by the queen, and the princess sat on a gold chair by Andrew. The queen gave Andrew a big red apple and some white cake.

"You will want to take off your cap when you eat," said the queen.

"Oh, no, no, no," said Andrew, "I can eat with my new red cap upon my head." And Andrew put both hands on his red cap.

"I will give you this pretty ring if you will give me your red cap," said the princess. And she showed Andrew a very pretty ring that was on her hand.

Andrew thought the ring was very pretty. He would have liked to show the ring to his mother.

"No, no," said Andrew, "I cannot give you my new red cap."

Just then the king came into the room.

"Father," said the princess, "this is Andrew, and he wants to show you his new red cap."

The king looked at Andrew, and he said, "Andrew, my boy, that is a very, very pretty red cap. I think I would like to have that red cap on my own head. How would you like to put on my gold crown?"

Andrew thought the king's gold crown was very pretty. He would have liked to show it to his father, but he could not give away the red cap his father had made.

"No, no, no," said Andrew, "I cannot give you my new red cap."

Andrew got down off the gold chair. He ran out of the room. He ran out of the palace. And he ran home just as fast as he could go.

"Father, Father!" cried Andrew. "The big boy said he would give me his cat for my red cap. The princess said she would give me her pretty ring for my red cap, and the king said he would give me his gold crown for my red cap. But I would not give away my red cap, because you made this red cap just for me."

The Gingerbread Boy

Once there was a little old woman and a little old man. They lived in a pretty little house. But no little boy lived with them. And no little girl lived with them. One day the little old woman said, "I will make a gingerbread boy." And that is just what she did.

The little old woman cut a boy out of gingerbread. She made him a cap and a coat out of gingerbread. She made him two eyes and a nose. Oh, my, what a pretty-looking gingerbread boy he was! Then the old woman put him into the oven.

Pretty soon the little old woman opened the oven door and looked into the oven. She wanted to see if the gingerbread boy was done.

"Let me out of here! Let me out of here!" said the gingerbread boy, and he jumped out of the oven.

"I am a little gingerbread boy. I am, I am. I can run away from you. I can, I can."

The little gingerbread boy ran out the door. And the little old woman ran after him. But she could not catch him.

The little old man was working in the garden. The gingerbread boy called to him as he ran, "I am a little gingerbread boy. I am, I am. I ran away from the little old woman. I can run away from you. I can, I can."

The little old man ran after the gingerbread boy. But he could not catch him.

The little gingerbread boy ran down the road. Soon he saw a brown-and-white cow eating green grass.

He called to the cow, "I am a little gingerbread boy. I am, I am. I ran away from the little old woman. I ran away from the little old man. I can run away from you. I can, I can."

The brown-and-white cow ran after the gingerbread boy. But she could not catch him.

The little gingerbread boy ran faster and faster. Pretty soon he saw a white pig eating corn.

The gingerbread boy called, "I am a little gingerbread boy. I am, I am. I ran away from the little old woman. I ran away from the little old man.

"I ran away from the brown-and-white cow. I can run away from you. I can, I can."

The pig stopped eating the yellow corn. He ran after the gingerbread boy. But he could not catch him.

"No one can catch me," laughed the gingerbread boy. And he ran away as fast as he could go.

Soon the gingerbread boy saw an old red fox. He called to the fox, "I am a little gingerbread boy. I am, I am. I ran away from the little old woman. I ran away from the little old man.

"I ran away from the brown-and-white cow. I ran away from the white pig. I can run away from you. I can, I can."

But the old red fox just went to sleep. The fox did not run after the gingerbread boy.

The little gingerbread boy stopped and called again to the fox, "You cannot catch me."

The old red fox just opened one eye and said, "What did you say? I cannot hear you."

The little gingerbread boy went right up to the fox.

The fox opened both his eyes. He gave one jump, and he ate the gingerbread boy all up.

"Oh no, oh no!" said the gingerbread boy. "Now I am all gone."

A Coin or Two

There was a town by the woods, far, far away. People who lived in this town worked and worked, but they could never get all the work done.

Once, just as the sun was going down, some people were walking together to town. One farmer said, "I will never get all my corn into the barn before the snow comes. My work is never done."

A man said, "Many people come to my store for bread, but I run out. I must have someone help me make bread."

"I have too many cows to milk," said someone. "I must have help milking the cows, or I will never be done."

In the woods a good-looking man could see the people. He could tell they wanted help. The man started to sing.

As the people were walking, they could hear the good-looking man singing in the woods, "Have you any work? Any work for me?"

They looked into the woods, and they did not see anyone. But they could hear him singing, "Have you any work for me? I will work for just a little."

People who were not walking came out of their houses. "We hear someone singing," they said. And they looked into the woods too.

Then the good-looking man walked from the woods singing, "I will work for just a little." And he looked like a man who could work and work!

"How much will you work for?" asked the farmer.

"Just a coin or two," said the good-looking man.

"I will give you a coin or two to work for me," said the farmer. "I will give you a coin or two to put all my corn in the barn."

"I will do it," said the good-looking man, "if you first put a coin or two into my red box."

"If I give you a coin or two first, how can I trust you to do the work?" asked the farmer.

"You can trust me," said the good-looking man. He said this with a warm laugh.

The laugh helped the farmer trust the good-looking man. "I will trust you," said the farmer as he put two coins into the red box.

Old Grandmother watched all this from down the street.

That night after the sun went down, the good-looking man started to work. He picked all the farmer's corn and put it into the barn. As he worked in the night, he laughed a warm, warm laugh. Not many people in the sleeping town could hear him laugh. But Old Grandmother did.

When the sun came up, all the corn was picked and in the barn. "You did it in one night!" the farmer said.

"Yes, I did," said the good-looking man with his warm laugh.

The farmer ran to the town to tell what the good-looking man had done.

"In one night the fool picked my corn and put it in the barn for a coin or two," said the farmer.

"He is a fool!" someone said.

Fool or not, the people wanted the good-looking man to work for them. They wanted him to make bread, milk cows, and clean houses.

"Where is the fool?" shouted the people to the farmer.

"He will be here as the sun goes down," said the farmer.

The people shouted, "We will be here!" Old Grandmother just watched.

When the sun went down, the good-looking man went into town. The people shouted, "Work for me! Work for me!"

"On paper, write down what you want me to do," said the good-looking man.

The people did. They handed the good-looking man the papers. He watched as the people put coins into his red box.

"I will work now," said the man. "Go to sleep, and your work will be done."

When the sun came up, the people looked around the town. No work was done! And the good-looking man was gone.

"He ran off with our coins," shouted the people. "He ran off with our coins."

"Who is the fool now?" asked Old Grandmother. "The man you all put so much trust in or each of you?"

"Each of us is a fool," someone said.

"Yes," said Old Grandmother.

Then she put the red box over her head. "But I got your coins back. The good-looking man was a fool, too, to sleep in the woods by the town."

The people shouted, "Thank you, Old Grandmother!"

And no one in town was a fool again— for a night or two.

The Rabbit That Was Afraid

Once there was a little rabbit that was afraid of everything. It was afraid of the wind and the rain. And it was afraid that the earth would break up.

"What shall I do when the earth breaks up?" cried the little rabbit. And the big rabbits always laughed at it.

One day the little rabbit was sleeping under a coconut tree. As the rabbit was sleeping, a big coconut fell from the tree. The coconut fell right by the rabbit.

The little rabbit jumped up. "Oh, oh, oh!" it cried. "The earth is breaking up. The earth is breaking up. What shall I do?"

The little rabbit jumped up and ran as fast as it could. It did not look back. It just ran and ran.

The little rabbit saw some big rabbits, and it cried, "The earth is breaking up! The earth is breaking up!"

The little rabbit was running so fast that the big rabbits ran after it.

Soon all the rabbits were running away together.

A deer saw the rabbits running. "Why are you running away so fast?" called the deer.

"The earth is breaking up!" cried the rabbits. "Come with us."

And the deer ran with the rabbits.

A fox saw them running. "Why are you running away so fast?" called the fox.

"The earth is breaking up!" cried the deer.

And so the fox ran with the deer and the rabbits. On and on they ran.

An elephant saw them running. "Why are you running away so fast?" called the elephant.

"The earth is breaking up!" cried the fox.

And so the elephant ran with the fox and the deer and the rabbits. They ran and ran and ran.

At last a lion saw all of them running. "Why are you running away so fast?" called the lion.

"The earth is breaking up!" cried the elephant.

The lion looked around. It did not see the earth breaking up. And so the lion roared. It roared three times. The elephant and the fox and the deer and the rabbits stopped.

The lion said, "Elephant, why are you running away so fast?"

"Oh, Lion," said the elephant, "the earth is breaking up."

"Who saw the earth breaking up?" asked the lion.

"I did not see it," said the elephant. "The fox said the earth was breaking up."

"I did not see it," said the fox. "The deer said the earth was breaking up."

"I did not see it," said the deer. "The rabbits said the earth was breaking up."

And the rabbits all looked at the little rabbit that was always afraid of everything.

"Little Rabbit," said the lion, "did you see the earth breaking up?"

"Oh, yes, Lion," said the little rabbit. "I was sleeping under a coconut tree. And the earth started to break up right there under the coconut tree. I ran away from there as fast as I could go."

"Then," said the lion, "you and I will go back to the coconut tree where the earth started to break up."

So the lion put the little rabbit on its back, and away they went.

They got to the coconut tree. The lion saw where the little rabbit had been sleeping. The lion saw the coconut in the grass.

"Oh, Little Rabbit," said the lion, "the earth is not breaking up. It was only a coconut that fell from the tree."

And then the little rabbit saw that it was silly to be afraid of everything.

Silly Jack

Once upon a time there was a boy named Jack. He lived with his mother. His mother worked all the time, but Jack was so silly that he did not work at all. All Jack did was play in the sun or sit by the fire and sleep.

One day his mother said, "Jack, you must go to work. If you want to eat, you must work."

And the day after that day, Jack went to work for a farmer.

And when the day was over, the farmer gave Jack some money. Jack had never had any money before, and he wanted to show it to his mother.

Jack went down the road carrying the money in his hand. Before long he lost the money. And when he got home and told his mother about the money, she said, "Jack, Jack, you lost the money because you carried it in your hand. You must carry things in your pocket."

"Carry it in my pocket," said Jack. "That is what I shall do."

And the day after that day, Jack went to help the farmer with his cows. And when the day was over, the farmer gave Jack some milk to take home.

Jack put the milk into his pocket and went down the road. And when he got home, the milk was gone.

"Oh, Jack," said his mother, "you lost the milk because you carried it in your pocket. You must carry milk in a pot on your head."

"Carry it on my head," said Jack. "That is just what I shall do."

And the day after that day, Jack went again to the farmer. And when the day was over, the farmer gave Jack some butter to take home.

Jack went down the road carrying the butter on his head. And when he got home, the butter had run down all over his eyes, nose, chin, and coat.

"Jack, Jack," said his mother, "why did you carry the butter on your head? You must carry butter in your hands."

"Carry it in my hands," said Jack. "That is just what I shall do."

The day after that day, Jack went to work for a baker. And when the day was over, the baker gave Jack a big black cat to take home.

Jack went away from the baker's house, carrying the big black cat in his hands. Pretty soon a dog ran up to them, and the black cat jumped out of Jack's hands.

"Oh, Jack," said his mother, "you lost the big black cat because you carried it in your hands. You must put a string around a cat, and then it will walk with you down the road."

"Put a string around it. Put a string around it," said Jack. "That is just what I shall do."

And the day after that day, Jack went to work for a butcher. And when the day was over, the butcher gave Jack some meat to take home.

Jack put a string around the meat and went down the road, pulling the meat by the string.

When he got home his mother said, "Jack, Jack, why did you pull that meat in the road? Now we cannot eat the good meat from the butcher. If you had carried the meat on your back, it would have been good to eat."

"Carry it on my back," said Jack. "That is just what I shall do."

And the day after that day, Jack went to work for a rich woman. This rich woman had a pretty daughter who had never laughed. And the rich woman had said that anyone who could make her daughter laugh could have a farm.

When the day was over, the rich woman gave Jack a little donkey.

Do you know what Jack did? He put that donkey on his back.

The daughter of the rich woman saw Jack going down the road with the donkey on his back. Jack looked so silly that she laughed and laughed.

The rich woman gave Silly Jack a farm, and Jack was never silly again.

The Three Little Pigs

There was once a mother pig who had three little pigs. One day the mother pig said, "Little pigs, the time has come for you to go and make houses of your own."

So the three little pigs went to make their own houses.

The first little pig saw a woman with some straw. The little pig said, "Please give me some straw so I can make a house of my own."

"Yes," said the woman, "I will give you some straw because you are a good little pig."

The first little pig made himself a house of the straw. And in no time at all, his house was done.

The second little pig saw a woman with some sticks. The little pig said, "Please give me some sticks so I can make a house of my own."

"Yes," said the woman, "I will give you some sticks because you are a good little pig."

The second little pig made himself a house of the sticks. And in no time at all, his house was done.

Now the third little pig saw a man with some bricks. The little pig said, "Please give me some bricks so I can make a house of my own."

"Yes," said the man, "I will give you some bricks because you are a good little pig."

The third little pig worked a long time. He made himself a house of the bricks.

The first little pig lived in the house of straw. The second little pig lived in the house of sticks. And the third little pig lived in the house of bricks.

One day a wolf came by the house of straw. "My, my," said the wolf to himself, "I smell a little pig."

The wolf went up to the door of the house made of straw and said, "Little pig, little pig, let me in. Let me in."

But the first little pig said, "I know you, old wolf. You want to eat me. No, no, no, I will not let you in. Not by the hair of my chinny, chin, chin."

"Then I will huff and I will puff and I will blow your house down," said the old wolf.

So the old wolf huffed and puffed, and he blew the house down. But the little pig ran out the back door. He ran as fast as he could to the second little pig that had the house of sticks.

And the old wolf did not get a little pig to eat that day.

One day the old wolf went by the house made of sticks. "My, my," said the old wolf to himself, "I smell two little pigs."

The old wolf went up to the door of the house made of sticks and said, "Little pigs, little pigs, let me in. Let me in."

But the two little pigs said, "We know you, old wolf. You want to eat us. No, no, no, we will not let you in. Not by the hairs of our chinny, chin, chins."

"Then I will huff and I will puff and I will blow your house down." So the old wolf huffed and he puffed and he puffed and he huffed and he blew the house down. But the two little pigs ran out the back door. They ran to the third little pig that had the house of bricks.

And the old wolf did not get two little pigs to eat that day.

One day the old wolf went by the house made of bricks. "My, my," said the old wolf to himself, "I smell three little pigs."

The old wolf went up to the door of the house made of bricks and said, "Little pigs, little pigs, let me in. Let me in."

But the three little pigs said, "No, no, no, we will not let you in. Not by the hairs of our chinny, chin, chins."

"Then I will huff and I will puff and I will blow your house down," said the old wolf. "I blew down the house of straw, and I blew down the house of sticks."

He huffed and puffed. But he could not blow down the house of bricks. He could not hurt the three little pigs that lived in the house of bricks. The old wolf sat down to think.

Then the old wolf called to the little pigs, "Little pigs, little pigs, I know where there are some turnips."

Now the little pigs liked turnips very much. "We would like some turnips," said the three little pigs.

The wolf laughed to himself.

"Farmer Smith has some big white turnips," said the old wolf. "I will come at six o'clock in the morning and show you where the turnips are."

But in the morning the three little pigs got up at five o'clock. They went to Farmer Smith's farm. They got a basket of big white turnips. Then they ran back to the little brick house.

At six o'clock the old wolf came by. He went to the door and called, "Little pigs, little pigs, let us go and get some turnips."

The little pigs said, "Go away, go away, old wolf. We have all the turnips we want."

The old wolf sat down to think. "Turnips are very good," said the old wolf, "but I like red apples too."

"And where are there red apples?" asked the three little pigs.

"Farmer Smith has some big red apples on his farm," said the wolf. "I will come at five o'clock in the morning and show you where the apples are."

The three little pigs liked to eat apples very much, and so they said, "Thank you, Wolf, for telling us about the apples. We would like some big red apples very much."

In the morning the three little pigs got up at four o'clock and went to Farmer Smith's farm.

In the morning the old wolf said to himself, "I think those three little pigs are going to get up at four o'clock. I will get up at four o'clock too. I will go right to Farmer Smith's farm."

When the old wolf got to Farmer Smith's farm, the three little pigs were up in the apple tree. They were picking big red apples and throwing them into their baskets.

"Good morning, little pigs," called the wolf. "Are the apples big and red?"

"Oh, yes," said the little pigs. "The apples are very good. We will get some apples for you."

The little pigs started to throw the apples as far from the apple tree as they could. When the wolf ran to get the apples, the three little pigs got down from the apple tree. They ran to the little brick house as fast as they could go.

The old wolf ran to the little brick house too. But the three little pigs got into the house before he got them. He jumped up and down and called to the three little pigs. "I will get you. I am going to eat three little pigs right away. I will come down your chimney right into your house. I will get you this time."

The wolf jumped and jumped. He jumped up to the top of the little house's chimney.

The three little pigs in the brick house worked very fast. The first little pig made a big fire. The second little pig got a big pot to throw on the fire. The third little pig put water into the pot. And the water got very, very hot.

When the wolf came down the chimney, he went right into the pot of hot water. The old wolf jumped out of the pot and ran out the door, and the three little pigs never saw him again.

And the three little pigs lived together in the little brick house a long, long time.

The Bear That Liked Music

Once there were two sisters who lived in the forest. One sister was always sad. Her name was Penny. One sister was always happy. Her name was Martha.

All day long Penny looked sad and did not say a word. Some days Penny went into the forest to cut wood.

As Penny cut wood, she looked sad and did not say a word.

Martha was always happy. She played a guitar and sang happy songs. And when Martha played her guitar, people were happy and danced.

Martha was good at working too. When she went to the forest to cut wood, she sang a happy song.

One cold day Penny went into the forest to cut wood.

As she worked, Penny looked sad and did not say a word.

A bear was sleeping in its den. Penny was making much noise cutting wood.

"Who is making all that noise?" roared the bear. "I cannot sleep with all that noise around me."

The bear came out of its den. It saw Penny cutting wood and looking sad.

The bear was very tired and not at all happy.

"Get out of my forest," roared the bear.

The bear ran at Penny. Penny was afraid and ran home as fast as she could go.

It was very cold, and there was no wood in the house. So Martha took her guitar and went to the forest. As she walked in the forest, she played her guitar and sang a happy song.

Martha found the wood Penny had been cutting.

Martha said to herself, "This is the wood Penny was cutting to put on the fire. I must take it home because the house is cold. But first I must sing a song."

Martha played on her guitar and sang a happy song.

"Who is making all that noise?" roared the bear. "I cannot sleep with all that noise around me."

The bear came out of its den. It looked around. It saw Martha playing her guitar and singing a happy song. The music was making the bear want to dance.

The bear danced and danced. At last it sat down.

"I like your music," said the bear, "and I like to dance. You may take the wood from my forest. I will not hurt you."

Then Martha carried the wood back to the house in the forest. She made a big fire.

Martha sat by the fire and played her guitar and sang a happy song. And Penny sat by the fire and looked sad and did not say a word.

The Coldest Time
of the Year

Once upon a time the tiger said to the bear, "The winter is the coldest time of the year."

"No, no," said the bear. "The coldest time of the year is when it rains."

"No, it is the wintertime," said the tiger. "Everyone knows that winter is the coldest time."

"No, it is coldest when it rains," said the bear. "Everyone knows that when you get wet, you feel cold."

The tiger and the bear saw a man in the forest. The tiger ran to the man.

"What is the coldest time of the year?" asked the tiger. "You must say the winter is coldest or I shall eat you."

The bear ran to the man.

"What is the coldest time of the year?" asked the bear. "If you do not say it is coldest when it rains, I shall eat you."

The man was afraid. He said, "I will tell you the time of the year I think is the coldest, but you must not eat me."

"Tell us!" said the tiger and the bear. Both of them thought they would eat the man if he did not say what he had been told to say.

The man said, "Would you say that the coldest time of the year is when you feel the coldest?"

"Yes," said the tiger.

"Yes," said the bear.

"It is very cold in the winter," said the man. "But your coat keeps you warm if the wind does not blow on you. You get wet when it rains, but you do not feel cold if the wind does not blow on you.

"It is the wind that makes you cold in winter. It is the wind that makes you cold when it rains and you are wet. I would say that the coldest time is when the wind blows and blows."

"Yes," said the tiger. "When the wind blows, I am cold."

"Yes," said the bear. "When the wind blows, I am cold. We had not thought of the wind."

The tiger did not eat the man. The bear did not eat the man. So the man went away.